The Power of Your Story
Participant Manual

# THE POWER
## OF YOUR STORY
*Participant Manual*

Rob Fischer

*with*

Cindy Crawford, Cindi Heath and Dianne Jongeward

Illustrations by
Jennifer Beecham Miller

The Power of Your Story
Participant's Manual

ISBN: 13: 978-1511742627

Interior layout by Kim Gardell

Cover design by Heather Wilbur

# TABLE OF CONTENTS

# FOREWORD

You're no doubt wondering why a man wrote a curriculum for post-abortive women. For me, it began nearly eight years ago when a friend shared a story with me and asked me to write a book telling the true stories of women who had experienced abortion.

At the time, I had no context or involvement with abortion or with women who had experienced abortion. Through a unique relationship with a crisis pregnancy center in Anchorage, Alaska, they put me in touch with 12 post-abortive women who were willing to bravely share their stories with me.

As they told their stories, I was humbled that they would take me into their confidence. Hearing and capturing their stories in print deeply moved and changed me. Previously, I had had no idea how devastating abortion could be in a woman's life.

Why would 12 women share their abortion stories complete with all the pain, trauma and chaos those abortions brought into their lives? Their overwhelming desire was to testify to the world how devastating abortion can be and to help other women begin to heal from their abortions. We agreed to tell those women's stories anonymously in the little book *13 Jars*.

Since writing *13 Jars*, I have heard the stories of many more post-abortive women and men.

Now, nearly eight years later, I find myself on the board of directors of Abortion Anonymous, Inc. (AbAnon), an organization whose mission it is to help post-abortive women and men recover from the emotional pain brought on by abortion.

You might find me an unlikely candidate to write a curriculum such as this. I've been married to the same woman, Linda, for over 40 years. We have three children, lost a fourth through miscarriage, and have nine wonderful grandchildren. I am passionate about helping post-abortive women and men on their journey toward healing.

I could not have written this curriculum without the help of the women whose stories are recorded in this work. Also, Cindy Crawford, Cindi Heath and Dianne Jongeward spent many hours poring over this curriculum to ensure its relevance and effectiveness for women like them who are post-abortive.

Because this curriculum is the joint work of these women and me, in many cases I've chosen to identify with you using the plural personal pronoun "we." Please accept my attempt to draw myself into your experience in this way.

We invite you to fully enter into this curriculum and the eight sessions you'll spend with other women like yourself. All sessions are gender-specific. I'm sure you'll meet some wonderful people and make some life-long friends in your AbAnon group.

Our hope and desire is that you will experience healing and a new-found hope through this curriculum!

—*Rob Fischer, November 2014*

# THE POWER
## OF YOUR STORY

*Participant Manual*

## SESSION ONE

WELCOME

_____ and _____ will be your facilitators for the next eight weeks. You are very courageous for taking this step toward processing your abortion. We're glad you're here.

INTRODUCTIONS

- Name
- Whatever you'd like to share with us to help us get to know you
- What would you like to take away from your experience over the next eight weeks?

## OVER THE NEXT EIGHT WEEKS, WE WILL TALK ABOUT

- Your abortion story
- How your abortion may have affected you
- Ways you may have coped with your abortion
- Your relationships
- Your child
- Common emotions surrounding abortion
- God & faith
- Healing & forgiveness

## ESTABLISH GROUP NORMS

We like to establish group norms or ground rules by which we agree to conduct our meetings together. This way we all have the same expectations and can get the most from this experience. Some group norms we see as essential are:

**Keep confidences**—What we say here stays here. We pledge to keep confidences and ask the same of each member of the group.

**Be present and ready**—Attend all the sessions (except in an emergency). Your presence here is not only important for you, but for the other participants as well. Being present includes keeping up with the light reading or homework between sessions.

**Be respectful**—We agree to respect each other: our individual situations, our ethnicity, our faiths, the choices we've made, the things we may say, how we each process our abortion.

**Function as a team**—We agree to function as a team: no one dominates the conversation; we listen to each other; we're here to assist, encourage and care for each other.

**Be humble**—We're not here to judge or *fix* each other. Sometimes the way we suppress our own need is by comparing ourselves to someone else or trying to fix them.

**What else** would you like to set down as a group norm?

## DISCLAIMER

We recognize that every person is different and working through issues surrounding your abortion usually occurs over time. Our sincere hope is that you will experience some measure of healing through this 8-week experience.

Also, we openly declare that our facilitators and co-facilitators are not professional counselors or life coaches. But having personally experienced an abortion, they are passionate about providing a safe, supportive environment for others.

Any profits from the sale of the Participant Manuals go to cover the cost of printing, shipping and the support and expansion of AbAnon. Abortion Anonymous, Inc. is a registered, 501c3 not-for-profit organization and is financed primarily through the generous contributions of donors.

If you are actively harming yourself or having suicidal thoughts, please seek the help of a professional counselor immediately. We can discretely help you locate a counselor if you like. This workshop is not intended to replace professional counseling or therapy.

## INTRODUCTION—THE POWER OF YOUR STORY

Welcome! We are so glad you've chosen to join us for this eight-week experience designed to help you process your abortion experience. Be assured that we will maintain the utmost confidentiality as you participate with this small group of women.

All of the facilitators or group leaders come with their own abortion stories and are in various stages of working through their abortion. Your facilitators are all volunteers and do not receive payment for leading a group.

The manual recognizes that although there are some basic issues that we all experience, or need to face, each woman processes her abortion in a different way. Some express the need for healing and others do not.

Whatever it is you seek with regard to your abortion, some sort of change is inevitable. Change can be difficult and scary, but necessary if we want to experience different outcomes than we're currently experiencing. Please avail yourself of every method and opportunity that we provide to help facilitate your desired change.

AbAnon is not an overtly religious organization and does not represent a particular religion, denomination or faith. Anyone, regardless of their faith or lack thereof, who has had an abortion experience is welcome to our gender-specific programs.

However, part of our 8-week program involves discussion about God, faith and forgiveness. Thousands of people have found change and healing through faith and we would be remiss in our responsibility if we failed to include God and faith in our curriculum.

Some of what we'll be discussing together will be inherently difficult to discuss, but remember, we're all in this together.


## HOW THE PARTICIPANT MANUAL WORKS

Each week or chapter has pre-work that you will complete *prior to* the next session. For instance, if you turn to Session Two in this Manual, you'll see that it begins with Cindy's Story, followed by some discussion questions and then a short reading on why it's so vital to share your story.

Some of the chapters also contain projects. Please do this homework early in the week so that you're not scrambling at the last minute to finish. Take your time and seek to gain all you can from this experience. The more you invest, the more you'll take away.

## ABORTION

We are here to acknowledge and empathize with you as you process your abortion experience. You are not alone.

In fact, according to the Guttmacher Institute, 21 percent of all pregnancies end in abortion in the US.[1] And between 35-40 percent of all women alive in the US today have had at least one abortion.[2] Each year, over 1 million abortions occur in the US. As of the writing of this curriculum in 2014, about 56 million abortions have been performed since its legalization in 1973.[3]

## POST ABORTIVE STRESS SYNDROME

Joan Appleton was the head nurse at Commonwealth [Abortion] Clinic. Joan was a very active member in the National Organization for Women (NOW). As a registered nurse, she felt she had a wonderful opportunity to practice and voice her beliefs in pro-choice.[4]

She was convinced that pro-choice was truly the best thing for women and began to work more and more with organizations like Planned Parenthood, NARAL and NAF. As a nurse she was issuing birth control pills to women after abortions and comments, "This is where I learned the real business, the real work of the abortion industry."[5]

Joan explains that abortion clinic workers handed out low-dose birth control pills with a high failure rate. They also neglected to tell women that taking a birth control pill while on antibiotics interferes with the action of the pill, making it useless. In this way, when their birth control failed, they were able to get more women to come in for abortions.[6]

Joan explains, "I often saw women who were injured emotionally by abortion. However, my supervisor told me, 'If she's having a problem after her abortion, it's because she was having a problem before her abortion.'"[7]

But it kept bothering Joan while she was head nurse at the clinic. "Why was it such an emotional trauma for a woman and such a difficult decision, if it was a natural thing to do? If it was right, why was it so difficult? I had to ask myself that all the time. I counseled these women so well, they were so sure of their decision. So why were they coming back now, months and years later, psychological wrecks?"[8]

Joan continues to explain that in the pro-choice movement and abortion industry, "We deny that there is any post-abortion syndrome. Yet it is real, and they do come back, and I couldn't deny their presence, and their numbers were increasing, and I kept asking, Why?"[9]

Joan soon realized that she wasn't helping women at all. Joan writes:

> If I was right, why are they suffering? What have we done? We created a monster, and now we don't know what to do with it. We created a monster so that we could now be pawns to the abortion industry, those of us women who really, really still believe in women's rights. Those of us who still believe in care and are pro-woman, who still believe that we are worth something, we are intelligent, we aren't doormats, we aren't something to be used, and we used ourselves. We abused ourselves.[10]

We refer to these very real psychological effects as Post Abortion Stress Syndrome (or PASS). Proponents of abortion often deny the existence of PASS. This brings additional pressure to bear on women who are feeling the negative effects of abortion, but are told that their feelings are not real or necessary.[11, 12]

However, Susanne Babbel, PhD, MFT, a psychologist specializing in trauma and depression has the following to say: "No matter your philosophical, religious, or political views on abortion, the fact of the matter is, the actual experience can affect women not only on a personal level but can potentially have psychological repercussions."[13]

Dr. Babbel goes on to explain:

> Post Abortion Stress Syndrome (PASS) is the name that has been given to the psychological aftereffects of abortion, based on Post Traumatic Stress Disorder (PTSD). It is important to note that this is not a term that has been accepted by the American Psychiatric Association or the American Psychological Association. Nevertheless, any event that causes trauma can indeed result in PTSD, and abortion is no exception.[14]

## PASS

How widespread is Post Abortion Stress Syndrome and the trauma on women (and men) brought on by abortion?

Nearly everyone agrees that feelings of loss and depression follow at some point after an abortion. Post Abortion Stress Syndrome (PASS) describes more severe and extensive trauma that may include:[15]

☐ Self-harm, strong suicidal thoughts or suicide attempts

☐ Increase in dangerous and/or unhealthy activities (alcohol/drug abuse, anorexia/bulimia, compulsive over-eating, cutting, casual and indifferent sex and other inappropriate risk-taking behaviors)

☐ Depression that is stronger than just 'a little sadness or the blues'

☐ Inability to perform normal self-care activities

☐ Inability to function normally in her job or in school

☐ Inability to take care of or relate to her existing children or function normally in her other relationships (i.e. with a spouse, partner, other family members or friends)

☐ A desire to immediately get pregnant and 'replace' the baby that was aborted.

In addition to the above, PASS sometimes does not appear until months or even many years after an abortion and may continue for months and even years. Other short- and long-term PASS symptoms may include:[16]

☐ Emotions, and dealing with emotional issues

☐ Anxiety and panic disorder

☐ Difficulty sleeping and sleeping problems

☐ Disturbing dreams and/or nightmares

☐ Problems with phobias, or increase in severity of existing phobias

☐ Repeated unplanned pregnancies with additional abortions

☐ Repeated unplanned pregnancies carried to term

☐ "Atonement marriage," where the woman marries the partner from the abortion, to help justify the abortion

☐ Distress at the sight of or socializing with other pregnant women, other people's babies and children

☐ Codependence and inability to make decisions easily

☐ Problems with severe and disproportionate anger

☐ Distress and problems with later pregnancy

☐ Added emotional issues and problems when dealing with future infertility or other physical complications resulting from the abortion

☐ Unhealthy obsession with excelling at work or school to justify the abortion

☐ Obsessive Pro-life or Pro-choice activism

☐ A lesbian lifestyle

## PASS SELF-ASSESSMENT

In your homework for next week, you will be asked to come back to these two lists of PASS symptoms in order to assess your own situation.

## WHERE DO WE GO FROM HERE?

Some of you may be thinking, "I've been trying to put my abortion behind me for years. Why would I want to revisit that experience again? I just want to put it behind me and forget about it." Others may be processing an abortion in a different way that's difficult to describe at this time. That's okay.

In the following seven weeks of *The Power of Your Story,* we want to join with you in processing your abortion. We'll provide you with tools and strategies for doing so. We want to help you find answers, support you, and offer you hope.

## HOMEWORK FOR THE NEXT SESSION

Please complete the tasks outlined in Session Two before our next session. You will find these on pages 21-34 in this manual. You may wish to turn there and go over these now.

## LOGISTICS

We'll meet here each week for seven more weeks at _____ (time).

## SESSION TWO

CINDY'S STORY

**Please read the following true story and reflect on the questions that follow.**

*During my childhood, my parents were very unhappy and fought all the time. They both worked hard but we had little money and they had difficulty communicating with each other. After years of fighting, they eventually divorced.*

*When I was 11, my father moved away. My mom went back to work and struggled to raise and feed my older brother, sister and me. As the youngest, I was a very fearful child and I spent a lot of time alone, worrying.*

*Not long after the divorce, my mom met and married a man. He had money and that helped our financial situation, but he was not a good person. When my mom married, my brother moved out, that left my older sister and me at home.*

*My step-father began to come into our rooms at night. My sister was 16 at the time and when he started to approach her sexually, she moved out. That left me, and for the next six years, my step-father sexually abused me.*

*My mom did not know what was happening. In fact, she seemed happy since she didn't have the financial stress anymore. I didn't tell anyone about what my step-father was doing to me. I was too ashamed and I wanted to keep peace in my family.*

*The abuse continued. He began to stop on back roads when we were driving somewhere, or if my mom was gone, he would find me at home. He began giving me gifts in a feeble attempt to placate me and keep me quiet.*

*You might wonder why I didn't say anything, but I felt like I had no way out. Who could I tell? By then he had moved us to a different city away from family and friends and away from my brother and sister. He built a beautiful home for my mom and me. To the people around us, we looked like a model family.*

*In order to cope, I began finding ways to stay busy and away from home. I often only came home from school if I had a friend with me. This way I didn't have to be alone with my step-father. My mom had gone back to school and got a job, so she was rarely home in the afternoons.*

*I felt trapped, insecure and lonely. I thought about telling my mom about my step-father, but deemed it risky because it would ruin our "family" and our security. I thought about confiding in someone else, but was afraid they wouldn't believe me, or worse that they wouldn't know what to do and leave me in my situation.*

*I desired acceptance and approval of others above all else and because of my fragile self-esteem, it felt safer to pretend and remain in shame and secrecy. I held back in my relationships with girlfriends, because I didn't want anyone to discover my secret. In my relationships with boys, I gave away too much because I wanted to be loved and secretly hoped that they might rescue me.*

*Since I was so needy and craved attention, I drove people away and my relationships were short-lived, leaving me to feel weak and abandoned again and again. This confirmed my biggest fear, that there was something wrong with me and I was not worthy of being loved.*

*The shame and insecurity increased. There seemed to be nowhere I could rest, nowhere I could be real and be loved unconditionally. I began to doubt that there was anyone that could truly love or accept me.*

*Time passed and my mom and step-father began to fight and our "fake" world began to crumble. After one awful night of fighting, my mom and I moved out and they divorced a short time later. By now, I was 16.*

*Living alone with my mom again, I wanted to keep peace in our home at all costs. She was healing from a divorce and I still felt somehow responsible for the abuse I had received from my step-father. I thought that by keeping my secret we would recover and move on with our lives. But many things had happened related to the abuse that I couldn't talk to my mom about until the truth came out.*

*One afternoon, I finally told my mom about the years of abuse, she listened and believed me. By telling her, my healing began. Somehow, the fact that one other person knew the truth released me and set me free. I was no longer carrying the burden of my abuse and shame alone.*

*I realize now that my secret only had power over me as long as it was kept hidden. My mom made me talk to a lawyer that day and started court proceedings against my step-father. This was very difficult for me.*

*It meant that secrets I had kept hidden for six years would be exposed—not only to my extended family but to strangers as well.*

*I found it embarrassing and humiliating to tell the jury the details of what my step-father had done to me. After the hearing, my step-father was sentenced to jail. It felt good that he was in jail, locked away and that I was now safe. Yet at the same time, I felt awful knowing that I was the one who put him there.*

*Looking back I know that standing up and telling the truth was the best thing I could do. This freed me from fear of him and living in shame. My secret lost its power when it was finally brought to light.*

*But the years after the hearing were difficult. I struggled to make new friends and start over. I was anxious to live a normal life but I didn't know what "normal" was. I had lived in dysfunction for so long, I didn't know what I was looking for.*

*During the years of my abuse, I had been invited to church with friends, but God felt distant to me. I still had so much shame and I was selective about with whom I'd share my story. I especially didn't want the truth of my past to come out in a church. It seemed like everyone at church had their lives together. They looked perfect from the outside and I was sure that nobody there had experienced what I had.*

*I also struggled with God. I wondered why He had abandoned me in my childhood. I wondered how a loving God could let this happen to me. I thought that maybe He was angry with me or didn't really care what had happened. I began to explore other religions and philosophies.*

*As I searched for answers, I sought security in relationships, education, and even food. I turned to anything that would distract and satisfy me, even if only temporarily. I continued to struggle with my deep desire to be accepted and loved.*

*While attending university, my roommate invited me to a Campus Crusade for Christ meeting where I met healthy-minded people. These were real people who had come through challenges in their lives and seemed happy and "normal." I wanted what they had. It was there that I learned about the unconditional love of God and how His Son, Jesus took all my sin on himself and all I had to do was believe and trust him so that I could be pure before God.*

*I saw this as my chance for a new life, a fresh beginning. Looking back, I realize that God was gently bringing me back to relationship with Him through this whole experience. I was hopeful for the first time in my life. I could start over. The only problem was I wanted his forgiveness, but I still wanted to control my own life. I wavered and now realize that I hadn't healed enough to handle what was coming next.*

*While in college, I began to date a guy I thought I would marry. Our relationship became serious very quickly. He was a paramedic and police officer and a nice guy—marriage quality—so I moved in with him. He did not share my new faith and I gradually grew away from God again.*

*Before long, I became pregnant. I was so excited because I thought that I was ready to start a new life as a wife and mother. I fully expected my boyfriend to accept my pregnancy and to marry me.*

*Unfortunately my boyfriend said he had no interest in becoming a father. We weren't married and he felt he had no obligation to stay with me. I had seen my mother struggle as a single mom. My dad had left me, my step-father abused me, and now I was feeling abandoned by a man again. I turned to family and everyone recommended abortion as my best option. I felt powerless and completely alone. I knew it was wrong but felt I had no other choice.*

*My boyfriend drove me to the clinic and paid for the procedure. When I got to the clinic, the waiting room was very quiet and all the other women were crying softly. When it was my turn to go back for the procedure, I remember the nurse saying it would be over quickly. I remember the suctioning. I remember asking her if it was a boy or a girl. She said, "It's pretty early to tell, but it looks like a boy."*

*She took me back to the waiting area and I began vomiting and crying. A wave of shame came over me very similar to the shame I had felt for years during my sexual abuse. I cried and a new emptiness filled my soul. I had taken God's gift, a child, and destroyed it. I knew this was wrong and I thought, "Now there's no way God will ever forgive me!"*

*I remember crying for two days straight, not wanting to get out of bed. My relationship with my boyfriend ended and I was left to sort through my messed up life again. I now felt further from God than I had as a child. Hopelessness filled my heart.*

*Over the next years, God tenderly called me back to himself through other Christians who loved and accepted me. But I never felt comfortable telling them my secret. I kept my abortion from them.*

*Then in 2009, I attended a conference where Francine Rivers spoke. She is an author that I had admired. She shocked me when she shared her abortion story. And I thought, "If she can share her story in front of a room full of women, then I need to come clean with some close friends of mine."*

*So I attended a post-abortive recovery group. I began to share more freely. Soon I began volunteering to help other women who were post-abortive.*

*As a child, I did not have a voice with my step-father who was abusing me. When I got pregnant, I felt that I had no voice with my boyfriend. I had felt censored; silenced by them. I had no other recourse, no power, no voice. Now, by sharing my story, God has redeemed my voice and taken away my awful guilt and shame.*

*—Cindy*

## DISCUSS CINDY'S STORY

1. In what ways can you identify with Cindy's story? What were you feeling?

2. In what ways did Cindy's abortion affect her?

3. What are you taking away from Cindy's story to help you process your abortion experience?

## WHY IT'S SO VITAL TO SHARE YOUR STORY

*The real freedom we seek is often found in the vulnerability of the secrets we least desire to talk about. – Lee Hudson*[17]

When interviewed, post-abortive women explained that sharing the personal story of their abortion was crucial to processing their abortion. An abortion often leaves a woman feeling "voiceless." That is, she may have been forced into the decision or felt coerced into it. But even if she made the decision to have an abortion willfully, she may have felt guilt and shame over it that left her *without a voice.*

*There truly is power in sharing your story.*

## HOW WE LOST OUR VOICE

Many women who have experienced an abortion express that they feel "voiceless." To be voiceless is to be powerless and vulnerable.

There are at least three ways that your abortion experience may have left you without a voice. First, many women feel deeply ashamed of their abortion. Shame causes us to hide what we've done. We live in fear of being found out or exposed. This fear prevents us from speaking the truth about our past and even may prompt us to lie about it. In this way, we feel *gagged* in terms of talking about our abortion.

Second, many women feel that they were coerced into their abortion. They believe that given the same chance again, they would not have chosen this path. Often, women were pressured, or forced to get an abortion by: the father of the baby, his parents, her parents, a sibling, well-meaning friends, a doctor, or social worker. In this case, someone else spoke on behalf of the woman and made the decision for her.

Finally, the voice of our culture speaks out in favor of abortion so loudly and pervasively that it overwhelms or drowns out our voice. For instance, the voice of the media and many people assert:

- "Abortion is a good choice."
- "You're doing the right thing to abort."
- "Abortion is perfectly safe."
- "Abortion is no big deal."
- "Abortion is the woman's right."
- "You have no other choice."
- "If it's legal, how can it be wrong?"
- "You're just not ready for children."

- "It's the socially responsible thing to do."
- "You can always have children later."

Because the voices who say those things are so loud and prevalent, we are made to feel ashamed that we feel differently and we are cowed into silence and stripped of our voice.

**Question:** To what extent do you feel you lost your voice in connection with your abortion experience? (Please circle your response.)

*Not at all      Perhaps a little      More than a little      To a great extent*

## HOW WE GAIN BACK OUR VOICE

To gain back our voice, we need to address each of the three ways above that may have left us voiceless.

First, there is a universal principle that helps us here: *Hiding our shame magnifies it and prolongs our agony. But when we reveal and renounce our shame, we find forgiveness and healing.* When we take the initiative to "come clean" and talk about what we did, we regain our voice.

It is said, "Confession is good for the soul." This is so true. One of the key steps for gaining back our voice and beginning our healing process is to share our abortion story with each other. We are not suggesting that you tell your story to just anyone, for not everyone will receive it well.

Many women feel that they need healing following their abortion, but that feeling sometimes does not surface until many years after their abortion. If you are one of those women, by sharing your story in a safe, caring environment, you will probably find release and a measure of healing.

Often, *the process of remembering is the beginning of healing.* This is because you are forced to recognize exactly what you're dealing with. Denying or ignoring any pain you might be experiencing from your abortion will only prolong your agony.

Coming to the point in which a woman reveals the secret of her abortion frees her spirit. What has been hidden is now in the open. Now she can speak. Getting your story "out in the open" (in the context of your AbAnon group) takes away some of the power from the guilt and shame you may have been feeling.

Second, if you feel you were in some way pressured or coerced into getting an abortion, you must denounce any victim mentality that remains. As long as we view ourselves as "victims" we remain powerless and voiceless. Victims remain victims. A victim cannot rise above their circumstances.

Third, recognize that although the voice of our culture and others may be loud this does not make them right. What the media or others declare does not necessarily express what you believe or are experiencing. You know what you feel. No one can argue with your experience. Take your voice back. Read back over this list of declarations. Take a few moments and reword each of these statements based on how you feel about your abortion today.

- "Abortion is a good choice."

- "You're doing the right thing to abort."

- "Abortion is perfectly safe."

- "Abortion is no big deal."

- "Abortion is the woman's right."

- "You have no other choice."

- "If it's legal, how can it be wrong?"

- "You're just not ready for children."

- "It's the socially responsible thing to do."

- "You can always have children later."

By telling your story, you give validity to the fact that your abortion experience significantly impacted your life. This is very important when so many are telling you to slough it off and forget about it. Others may say, "It's no big deal," but if it has been troubling to you, then sharing your story will validate what you've been feeling.

## SHARING YOUR STORY

There are also several other reasons to share your abortion story—especially in the context of a safe, caring environment like we seek to provide in your AbAnon small group.

First, hearing other women's stories may encourage you that you're not alone. There are many other women who have experienced similar things. They understand what you're going through. They can empathize with you. They've experienced things like: confusion, inner turmoil, shame, guilt, grief, or pain.

Second, as you hear others' stories, you may realize things that you hadn't thought of before. Hearing their experiences may help you identify past (and perhaps present) behaviors that may be harmful.

Third, hearing other women's stories will no doubt evoke compassion in you and allow you to extend grace and understanding toward them and receive it yourself. While being transparent and gracious with each other, we learn to be gracious in our other relationships as well.

Fourth, sharing your story with this small group of women will hopefully help you bond with them and deepen your relationships with them.

Finally, as you share your story and hear the other women in the group tell their stories, you will experience the power of standing together. We were never meant to try to struggle through life alone. We need each other. Take advantage of this tremendous support system being made available to you.

## TAKE ACTION: PASS SELF-ASSESSMENT AND WRITE YOUR STORY

### PASS Self-Assessment

Take a few moments and go over the two PASS lists in the material on pages 17-19. Check any of those symptoms that you have experienced in the past or are experiencing now. This exercise is for your eyes only, so please be completely honest with yourself.

It's important for us to recognize that these lists represent *symptoms* of a root issue and not the issue itself.

## WRITE YOUR STORY

Below are some questions you may want to consider when writing your story.

1.  How old were you when you had your abortion?

2.  What factors led to your abortion?

3.  Describe the relationship you were in that led to your pregnancy.

4.  What were your goals and aspirations at the time you got pregnant?

5.  Who influenced your decision to abort your child?

6.  What was happening when you went for the abortion?

7.  What do you remember about the abortion procedure itself?

8.   How did you feel immediately following the abortion? Where did you go? What did you do? Who were you with?

9.   In what ways has your abortion affected your life since it occurred?

10.   What else would be helpful for you to either get off your chest or share for someone else's benefit?

## SESSION THREE

MARIE'S STORY

**Please read the following true story and reflect on the questions that follow.**

*At age 11, my parents divorced. They had fought a lot and my dad, a former Marine, was physically and verbally abusive toward my mom. He also habitually touched me inappropriately. When we called him on it, his military, "stuff your feelings" attitude was forced upon us.*

*I grew up going to church with my mom. I read the Bible, tried to make good choices, and dreamed of one day getting married and having a family.*

*I didn't date a lot. Perhaps my religious upbringing intimidated the boys. I remember finding out that an unwed older girl in church had gotten pregnant. I couldn't believe how any Christian could do such a thing and I judged her harshly for it.*

*When I was 15, I met Glenn at a roller skating rink. He too was being raised by a single mom. His mom drove truck, so she was gone a lot. Glenn was always in trouble at school, but he was sweet, responsible and attentive to me. I was impressed with his knowledge and ability to talk. Glenn was not a Christian. He pursued me and we eventually started dating.*

*Glenn didn't go to church on his own, but as we began seeing each other, he tagged along with me on Sundays. I had lots of boundaries imposed on me from my mom and church, but Glenn had very few.*

*We dated for two years and spent a lot of time together. My mom trusted me and his mom didn't care. Because both our mothers worked, we spent way too much time alone and became sexually active. At first this was strictly taboo for me.*

*I cried after the first time we made love. I felt like I had just forfeited something precious I could never get back. Gone was the hope of a beautiful wedding in a white gown, followed by the enchantment of the honeymoon night discovering each other for the first time.*

*But after having sex once, I became addicted and we had sex all the time in the absence of our moms. Glenn and I went to different high schools and he would pick me up after school so we could be together. As far as birth control was concerned, we occasionally used a condom, but mostly just the "pull-out" method. We were very naïve and thought we would never get pregnant.*

*After about six or seven months of being sexually active I became pregnant. My period was late and I got scared. I tried not to have sex, but I couldn't stop. I was in denial about being pregnant, but finally took a pregnancy test at home and tested positive. I hid it from my mom.*

*I told Glenn and he and I went to two or three clinics, not knowing what to do. At the first clinic, a woman gave me another pregnancy test to confirm my pregnancy. She asked me, "Would you like to see what your baby looks like at this stage of its development?" But I didn't want to see. I was still in denial about the whole thing and tried to shove it down.*

*Then we went to the Catholic Charities and they walked through all of our options with us, including adoption. But because of Glenn's upbringing, he was against adoption and didn't want to deal with what he perceived might happen with the child.*

*We didn't like the various options presented to us by the Catholic Charities because they all involved owning up to what we had done. We wanted to keep this quiet at all costs. I knew my mom would kill me if she found out and I couldn't imagine the shame of being exposed at church. I was serving then as the vice-president of our youth group.*

*Finally, we felt like we had no choice other than abortion. Glenn and I went to Planned Parenthood and met with a representative in an open cubicle. I had seen a girl from one of my classes at school in the waiting room and was concerned about the lack of privacy in this cubicle. Everyone could hear what was being said in the various cubicles and I didn't want that girl to know why we were there.*

*The woman at Planned Parenthood asked me how far along I was and I told her 10 or 11 weeks. I had been in denial about my pregnancy, that's why I waited so long. She gave us the name and address of a doctor and told us it would cost about $325.*

*We made an appointment with the doctor and went in for a consultation. He was very cold and all business. I remember there were no windows at this facility and there was no caring there. It didn't feel right.*

*A few days later, my mom—who was still unaware that I was pregnant—dropped me off at school. Glenn and I had arranged that he would swing by and pick me up right after she let me off. He and I drove to a fast-food restaurant and waited there until my appointment. I had forged a note to the school from my mom explaining my absence. This was April of our senior year.*

*There we were, two high school students by ourselves making choices we should never have made. I had told Glenn that the only way I'd go through with the abortion was if he stayed by my side the whole time and he agreed to do so.*

*At the doctor's office, I paid for the abortion out of my own savings hoping that my mom wouldn't find out. Glenn and I were led into a room where the procedure was to be performed. The doctor coldly told us what to expect. The room felt surgical and unfriendly. Both the doctor and nurse were void of caring. Nothing felt normal. I had to detach myself from it all. I had always dreamed of having children, and now this…*

*I remember the horror of hearing and feeling the vacuum and the scraping of instruments inside me. At one point the doctor broke an instrument in my womb. He became very angry and upset. I had blocked out this memory, but Glenn described it to me later.*

*After the abortion, we went down the hall to a back room and I was afraid I would pass out. I did get sick and threw up in the hallway. The nurse wasn't happy with me for doing that. She put me in a room and told me to get dressed, but I couldn't function. Glenn had to help me dress. Then the nurse talked to me about pain killers.*

*We stopped at a drugstore on the way home and filled a prescription for medication. The next day I had cramps and was sick so I stayed home from school again—it was a Friday. All weekend was a blur. I felt empty and knew that what I had done was very wrong. I was overwhelmed with grief and shame.*

*On Sunday, Glenn told me he was going skiing with friends and I was angry at him for leaving me alone. I had no one else to be with. I went to church, but it was very hard being there.*

*For several days, Glenn and I didn't talk. I couldn't eat and my mom and one of my teachers became very concerned about me. I was moved that they cared for me.*

*A week or two later at school, I ran into the girl who had seen me at Planned Parenthood. She commented that she had overheard someone talking about getting an abortion. I snipped back her, "I can't imagine anyone ever doing that!"*

*When I had gone in for the abortion, the doctor had asked about birth control and I told him we didn't need any. And a couple weeks after the abortion, Glenn and I began having sex again. We planned to get married right after graduation. Shortly before school ended I became pregnant again.*

*"How could this happen to me again!" I had a graduation and a wedding to plan. Glenn and I graduated and got married a week later. The week after our wedding, Glenn left for basic training in the military.*

*My mom still didn't know about my pregnancy and again I was in denial about it. But Mom noticed I wasn't having my period and asked me. I told her I was pregnant, but just wasn't ready yet to deal with a baby. To my utter shock she said, "There's a simple procedure to take care of that."*

*Perhaps in a subconscious effort to starve myself and the baby, I deprived myself of food and water during this time.*

*Now that Glenn was in the Air Force, I could go to the base for my medical needs. We made an appointment with a doctor on base and I went to see him. Reluctantly, I admitted to him that I had had an abortion in April and that I wasn't sure I wanted this baby either. I was scared.*

*This doctor was very kind. He noticed the cross on my necklace and asked me about its significance. I told him that it represented Christ's death on the cross for me and that I had received him as my Savior. Then the doctor gently told me that having an abortion would not be good for me.*

*He also warned me that unless I started eating and drinking water he would have to hospitalize me and that charges could be brought against me for neglecting my unborn child. I realize now that this was an empty threat, but it had the desired effect. I truly believe this doctor saved my life. I had been so depressed that I may very well have taken my life if things had not changed.*

*Up until now, my mom thought I had gotten pregnant on our wedding night, but when I told her my due date she came unglued. She was very upset and horrified about what people at church would think. Then my mom had a change of heart and decided to take me out for a steak to celebrate the coming of her grandchild.*

*Over the next months, my relationship with Glenn grew very tenuous. His mom pitted him against me and my mom did the same with me toward him. At one point, we both hired lawyers and were heading toward divorce. But I still loved Glenn and so I called him behind my mother's back. He and I agreed to meet and talk things out. We decided to stay together and work on our marriage, but the next several years were very rocky. We often sought counsel with various pastors to help us in our marriage.*

*Glenn and I moved to Tacoma, WA, and there our son, Mark was born. I felt like Mark had saved my life from the grief of my abortion. But it was wrong of me to place that burden on him.*

*By the time Mark was five, I wanted another baby—hoping for a girl, but Glenn couldn't see how we would manage. However, we agreed to "let things happen" and they did. I eventually got pregnant and we had little Robin.*

*Robin was extremely fussy and colicky from the start. Something was wrong, but I couldn't convince the doctors of it. She couldn't keep anything down. She was failing to thrive. I finally found a doctor who listened to me and we were able to get Robin on a new formula that her system could handle and she began to sleep and play normally.*

*After 10 years we moved. Glenn was gone a lot, I had no family in this new town and year after year I seemed to grow more depressed. At times I contemplated suicide.*

*Meanwhile, Mark seemed to have a serious anger issue, so I went to see our pastor about Mark's anger, while burying my own. During that session, I confessed to my pastor that I had had an abortion. He referred me to a woman who could help me. We met and she shared with me about her abortion and how she had finally come to the place where she could forgive herself.*

*Forgiving myself for what I had done was inconceivable to me and I expressed that to her. In reply, she asked, "Are you more worthy than God?" Meaning, "God forgives you. Are you more holy than He is that you cannot forgive yourself?" She then encouraged me to attend a group going through a post abortive recovery experience called PACE.*

*I attended and began my journey toward healing. I learned that God invites us to call him "Abba," which means "Daddy." He became the loving father to me that I never had. This occurred about 14 years after my abortion. I also learned that healing from an abortion doesn't usually occur all at once. It is often a lengthy process that God leads us through over many years.*

*During PACE, they challenged us to ask God the gender of our aborted child and to name the child. Before this, I had never wanted to know its gender, but I prayed. Shortly thereafter I had a dream in which a little girl ran toward me with outstretched arms. She looked just like Mark, which puzzled me, and I knew this wasn't Robin. When I woke up,*

*I realized that God had answered my prayer and revealed to me that my baby had been a girl.*

*Later, I told Mark about my abortion and then about this dream. With childlike wisdom he said, "What about naming her Grace?" And I knew that was her name! Through all this I experienced God's love for me and he began restoring my joy.*

*A few years later, with my husband's support I began volunteering at a pregnancy center sharing my story and helping young pregnant girls and women who are post-abortive. God continues to heal me 30 years after my abortion.*

*—Marie*

## DISCUSS MARIE'S STORY

1. In what ways can you identify with Marie's story? What were you feeling?

2. What did Marie do to process her abortion?

3. What can you take away from her story that may help you heal?

## FOR MANY, ABORTION IS AN ACT OF DESPAIR

Consider that for many women, abortion is an act of despair. A girl or young woman who discovers she's pregnant may feel trapped and that there's no way out. She may not have intended to have sex in the first place, but caved to the persistence of a boyfriend who said he loved her. In some cases she may have been raped. Either situation can magnify her sense of despair in the face of an unwanted pregnancy.

Whatever the situation, a woman may now feel caught in a trap with no escape. Added to this is the all-too-frequent scenario that the boyfriend wants nothing to do with a baby, and he may even reject her now because she's become a "problem." She's convinced that her life (as she knows it) will end if she has this baby.

So, it's the desperate choice of *her* life or that of a nameless, genderless, faceless child within her.

Frederica Mathewes-Green of Feminists for Life of America describes the despair that many women feel when deciding to abort, "No woman wants an abortion as she wants an ice cream or a Porsche. She wants an abortion as an animal caught in a trap wants to gnaw off its own leg."[18]

In such a case, her decision is fraught with despair. Her maternal instincts and hormones have already begun to influence her physically and emotionally. But she's torn because she sees this unexpected pregnancy as the end of all she's planned and hoped for. She desperately wants things back "the way they were."

She may *agonize* over the decision whether to have an abortion. The fact that her conscience is active and tormenting her over the decision, may lead her to rationalize that the pain of the struggle itself makes it morally acceptable.

However, most women who have abortions do so believing it is morally wrong.[19] But at this point, in despair and hopelessness, many women capitulate—defying their conscience and values. In a state of shock they numbly go through the motions of the abortion. Often, even while lying on the operating table, they are screaming inside, "My God, what am I doing!"

But it's too late. The deed is now done. And the despair that drove them to abort isn't gone! Oh, she may feel relief at first; many women do. But months or years later, the despair, like an angry ravenous beast, has now feasted on the abortion and rises to greater strength to consume her as well.

This beast of despair now snarls at the woman, "You are such a horrible person! Look what you've done, taking the life of your child! You are worthless, good for nothing and fit for no one!"

In her despair, she believes the accusations and slandering of this beast. She believes she is unworthy of love. She thinks, "God could never forgive me." "God will never trust me with children again." "I don't deserve anything good." And she begins living out this desperate life that she now envisions for herself.

She may try to medicate or subconsciously punish herself with drugs, alcohol, food, or unbridled sexual escapades. Or she may try to stuff her despair by burying herself in a career or some extreme hobby—anything to take her mind off the abortion and her despair. Some women become self-destructive, contemplating suicide and even attempting it. Any of these efforts will only intensify despair, increasing its downward spiral.

In fear and anguish, the woman now reflects on those who coerced her, urged her, "supported" her, or merely failed to challenge her in her decision to abort, and she *despises* them. If a woman felt alone before the abortion, now she may feel totally isolated and alienated from others.

All of this may be very painful for some who are reading this. If *despair* led you to abort, then *despair* will prevent you from healing. The question is how do we replace despair with hope?

## REPLACING DESPAIR WITH HOPE

If the above describes you, there are at least four things you can do to destroy this beast of despair in your life. **First**, recognize that the accusations of this beast are false. They are lies. Even though you may now believe your abortion was wrong, the abortion does not diminish your worth as a person, or as a woman.

Your worth is not measured by what you've done or haven't done, but by who you are. You are a beautiful daughter, a lovely creation.

**Second**, identify and reject self-destructive behaviors. You cannot "pay" for what you did or what you allowed to happen to your child. Your child would not want you hurt. Harming yourself in any way will only bring you and those you love more misery, hopelessness and pain. Instead, seek those habits, behaviors and thoughts that are wholesome, healthy and promote hope.

A great way to instill hope is to provide hope to others by serving them. Perhaps you could look for ways to help other post-abortive women; volunteer at a charity; or help the homeless. Serving others may seem like the last thing you'd want to do right now. But experience shows that serving others is very therapeutic. Build your life around positive, healthy people and practices.

**Third**, strive to let go of anger and bitterness and seek to forgive others. When an animal is injured in the wild, it often crawls off to die alone. Because we feel wounded, we may be tempted to do the same. Being angry and bitter toward others fuels our imagination with evil thoughts about them and drives us into isolation and loneliness. We'll talk more about relationships and forgiveness in a later chapter.

**Fourth**, draw near to others who love you deeply—in spite of your abortion. Their love substantiates that you are lovable. You were created to love and to be loved. You are worthy of good and capable of wonderful things. Accept their love and let it fill you with hope for a brighter future.

## TAKE ACTION

1.  Look back over those four ways above of replacing despair with hope mentioned above. Which ones will you begin to put into practice this week? How will you do that?

2.  Go somewhere quiet and alone. Hold a mirror up to your face. Look beyond the reflection you see in the mirror and identify at least 10 positive attributes about yourself. List these positive attributes here and state them in this fashion: "I am _____."

    a.

    b.

    c.

    d.

    e.

    f.

    g.

    h.

    i.

    j.

**SESSION FOUR**

SANDI'S STORY

**Please read the following true story and reflect on the questions that follow.**

*I was raised in a religious home, but one in which we never opened a Bible, talked about our faith, or prayed. We were what you might call "Christian-lite"—where we had a form of Christianity, but lacked its substance and power.*

*So it was, at about age 15, I began slipping morally and by college was into a full downward slide. When I was still a young girl in junior high, I had been quite a provocative dresser. What disturbed me and really sent me mixed messages was that my mother encouraged this. She seemed to want to relive her youth through me and direct my life toward her version of being attractive to men. Having a man was primary to her and she wanted to make sure I attracted one.*

*This approach worked all too well as I remember being openly propositioned by three grown men during my teen years. One was a teacher, then a school counselor, and finally a policeman who promised me special immunities if I played along with him. I didn't yield to any of their propositions, although there was some kissing in one case.*

*The sexual advances of these three men in leadership roles and the mixed messages I received from my mother left me with little trust or respect for authority. This made me feisty and brazen. As a result, in junior and senior high, I had an unearned reputation about my morals and sex life. There were all sorts of rumors about the kind of girl I was, even though at the time I was still a virgin.*

*In my senior year of high school my mom took me to a routine appointment with a gynecologist. While there, she told me in his presence, "You should get birth control pills." Both the doctor and I were stunned that she would encourage this. The doctor tried to dissuade my mom, but she won out and he prescribed the pill.*

*Meanwhile, I had hooked up with a guy from our neighborhood who was three years older than I. Before I started on the pill, I found out I was pregnant. My boyfriend told his dad and his dad asked him if he wanted to marry me. My boyfriend proposed and I said, "No."*

*Abortion had just recently been made legal, so I didn't give it another thought. I just did it. Deep down inside I think I knew that this was more than "tissue," but I was pretty stoic about it. I didn't trust my parents, so I didn't tell them about my abortion.*

*All during these years, I maintained a façade of Christianity, but was greatly disillusioned by what I saw. For instance, our pastor's daughter had already had two abortions and the choir director's daughter had one as well. Like most children, I could not bear hypocrisy and theirs was blatant! Because of all this, I didn't think much about my abortion at all.*

*I started college and fell in love with a guy. But I soon became very ill. We couldn't figure out what was wrong with me. The doctors subjected me to all kinds of tests and put me on some heavy-duty drugs. Due to some possible drug interactions, they took me off birth-control meds. Finally, they discovered that I had a very serious kidney infection.*

*As this was going on, I had gotten pregnant again. This time I planned to keep my baby, but the doctor convinced me to abort. He counseled that with my illness and the drugs I had been taking, there was the possibility of deformities.*

*When I told my boyfriend I was going to have an abortion, he was disappointed and disapproved. He went to the clinic with me, only because he loved me. For me at the time, this abortion was merely a logical decision. My boyfriend and I never talked about the abortion again. We had gotten engaged, but never married due to friction with his family.*

*A few years later, I met a man who had a three-year-old daughter. When we married, we both agreed we didn't want any more children. With time I fell in love with his little girl and desired children of my own. He refused to have children with me, so I walked out of the marriage.*

*By the time I was 26 years old, I thought I would not remarry. I had wandered very far from God and was trying to be an agnostic. For 20 years I was on the run. I didn't like or trust God and I was trying very hard to be bad.*

*After my divorce, I intentionally got pregnant and carried my child to term. I had a little girl. During the pregnancy, I often wondered, "Why would God allow me to have a child when I had aborted my first two children?"*

*After my daughter was born, I got married and had a second baby—a boy with a severe heart disorder. On the day that I found out about his heart, I left the hospital and sat in my car and cussed God out. I was so angry at Him for allowing this. What I said to Him was horrible. The irony of my little "chat" with God was that it demonstrated my acknowledgement of Him. I have always known that God was thinking something like, "Well, at least she's talking to me now."*

*Largely due to what I was experiencing with my son, I began dabbling in church again. One Sunday—as weird as it sounds—I had some kind of vision having to do with water. I had no idea what it meant, but it really plagued me. I was so perplexed about it that I went home and spent many hours into the night poring over the Bible trying to figure out what it meant.*

*Then, I happened on an obscure passage in Jeremiah 1:5, "I knew you before I formed you in your mother's womb. Before you were born I set you apart and appointed you as my prophet to the nations." And for the first time, reading that verse, I realized that I had murdered my first two babies. I fell on my face crying out to God, confessing my sin and repenting for what I had done.*

*On the spot, God delivered me from all my sin, guilt and shame. Through my complete awareness of what I'd done, coupled with confession and repentance, God delivered me and gave me a sense of freedom like I had never felt before in my life. This was 23 years ago.*

*I realize that many other women struggle with their healing for years, but it was not like that for me. God took it from me in an instant. He knows how to reach each of us personally to draw us back to Him and help us heal.*

*Ever since then, I've served as a pro-life advocate in any way I can. One time I was working a pro-life booth at a State Fair. We had little models laid out on the table illustrating the stages of a baby's development from conception to nearly full-term.*

*A handsome couple walked up and began moving down the table. I was especially drawn into the expressions on the face of the man. He was staring at these models of fetal development. As they worked their way down the table, his facial expression changed until it grew dark and hardened.*

*Then he asked one of my co-workers, "Are these for real?" She replied, "Yes, they are." At that, this man's eyes filled with tears and he said, "They lied to us!"*

*I'm 61 now, but I lost 20 years of my life running from God and doing my own thing. I lived a very rough life. Many people have told me, "We can't believe you're still alive." But I discovered that during those 20 years, my girlfriend's grandmother prayed for me. She prayed for me all the time. I know that's why I came out of my 20-year rebellion alive.*

*—Sandi*

## DISCUSS SANDI'S STORY

1.  In what ways can you identify with Sandi's story? What were you feeling?

2.  What did Sandi do to process her abortion?

3.  In what ways does reading Sandi's story give you hope and comfort?

## REGRET AND YOUR BABY

Regret is another emotion that many women manifest to express the *pain* of their abortion. We all have past regrets. Regret is sorrow over things we've done that we wish we hadn't; and things we didn't do, but wish we had.

Women commonly express a number of regrets around their abortion. Look at the list on the following page and check all the boxes that apply to you.

I regret that…

☐ I was even dating that guy.

☐ I had sex at the time.

☐ I got pregnant in the first place.

☐ I listened to those who urged me to get the abortion.

☐ I didn't listen to those who tried to dissuade me from having an abortion.

☐ My boyfriend, husband, father, mother, sibling or someone else close didn't keep me from aborting my child.

☐ I had the abortion.

☐ I didn't let my baby live.

☐ I don't know my baby, its gender, or anything else about him/her.

☐ Other: _____

_____

Much like the other emotions many women feel as a result of their abortion, regret prevents us from moving past our grief. One reason that regret is so debilitating is that it is based on something that happened in the *past*. The problem is we cannot change the past. So, to continually live in regret over our past abortion is futile—and cannot help us get beyond it.

We carry regret around like too much baggage. This baggage encumbers us and weighs us down. No matter where we go, we find ourselves dragging this heavy load with us. Sometimes the emotional strain we feel under this burden is unbearable. Yet we feel torn. On the one hand, we wish we could discard this great burden, and on the other hand we feel that we dare not part with it.

So it is with the regrets around our abortion. We feel terrible about our abortion and know that we must never deny the gravity of what we've done. But we wish we could somehow shed some of its weight. Consequently, in some measure there will always be feelings of regret. But too much regret can weigh us down, crushing us under its weight and making life a constant struggle.

We experience waves of remorse, sorrow, and grief over what we've done *and* what was done to us. We have an unquenchable longing to somehow miraculously undo what was done—*but we can't*. At times we may get caught in the whirlpool of "What ifs" around our whole abortion experience. But going there only stirs up *more* regret.

The regret we feel is often tied directly to our baby. Before our abortion, our culture and others around us may have led us to think about our baby in the following terms:

- Depersonalized
- Dehumanized ("It's just tissue")
- Removed or distant
- Surreal, or unreal

But at some time after our abortion we may experience:

- Reality set in about our baby—it was a human being, a person

- We desire to know about our baby—its gender, hair and eye color, etc.

- We may fantasize about our baby and what he or she would have been like

As we mentioned, regret, sorrow and grief are all forms of emotional pain. As with physical pain, pain plays an important role in letting us know "something is wrong." As such, there are only two primary responses to pain: we can either suppress it, or take steps to cope with it.

While suppressing the pain may be a coping mechanism, it's not a good one, because it doesn't solve anything. Suppressing or ignoring regret and sorrow, though common, is an irrational response that will result in abnormal behaviors leading to more regret.

Instead, we must take steps toward coping effectively with our regret. We offer three steps here, but you may discover other steps as well.

1. **Lay down the baggage of "what ifs" and second guessing.** You cannot change the past no matter how badly you wish you could. Settle that in your mind and unload that burden from your shoulders.

   *God grant me the serenity to accept the things I cannot change, the courage to change the things I can, and the wisdom to know the difference.* — *Reinhold Niebuhr*

2. **Discard the baggage of things you could not control.** No doubt there were circumstances around your abortion over which you had no control. If so, you are carrying someone else's baggage. Release it and be free from it.

3.  **Set down that trunk full of old tapes that you carry around with you and keep replaying.** You know the tapes that I'm referring to: they are reruns of your whole abortion experience. These may include conversations, people you'd rather forget, the cold clinic, the noises and smells. Shut them all tight in that trunk and push it off the end of a dock into the depths of the ocean. Be done with it.

Yes, there will always be a reasonable amount of regret attached to your abortion, but learn to travel light when it comes to regret.

## TAKE ACTION

Please take time to get alone and walk through those three steps for coping with regret. Visualize yourself laying down the weighty burden of each one. Take your time. Make sure you really do put it down and walk away from it. Record here for future reference what you did with each of these burdens.

1. Lay down the baggage of "what ifs" and second-guessing.

2. Discard the baggage of things you could not control. Rid yourself of the burden of someone else's baggage.

3. Set down that trunk full of old tapes that you carry around with you and keep replaying. Then push that trunk off the end of a dock into the deep ocean.

4. Finally, is there another heavy piece of baggage that we did not identify that you can also lay down? If so, write that down here and take steps to abandon it like the others.

## SESSION FIVE

DIANNE'S STORY

**Please read the following true story and reflect on the questions that follow.**

*My boyfriend, Dave, and I had been dating for a year-and-a-half when I got pregnant. When I told him the news, he panicked. Without asking, he made an appointment at an abortion clinic and called to let me know.*

*My world was crushed! The man, who I thought loved me, was unwilling to do the right thing. We had talked about marriage and I had been anticipating a proposal in the near future.*

*As Dave drove me to the clinic I was consumed with fear and felt pressured to follow through with the abortion. I wanted to talk to my best friend to get her advice, but I was too ashamed and afraid. I felt I couldn't talk to anyone.*

*As a Christian, I was already carrying the shame of being pregnant out of wedlock. While I bought into the then popular claim that my baby was just tissue, deep down I questioned whether that was really true.*

*I was very afraid. Everyone that day was telling me that everything would be fine.*

*Lying on the table with the doctor's wife holding my hand, I was dying inside. I felt overwhelmed with guilt, and then ... it was too late! I was devastated and filled with regret.*

*Still lying on the table, I began sobbing and begging God to forgive me. The nurse tried to console me saying, "Everything's alright." And I remember telling her, "No! Everything is not alright!" I had been deceived. I had been lied to. I felt like I had been thrown to the wolves. I was just a dollar sign to them. I left that place empty; a broken woman.*

*I was in shock and in mourning. But I plastered on a fake smile and pretended to my family and friends that all was good.*

*Dave and I stayed together as a couple, even though our relationship was now anything but healthy. I still loved him, but I hated what he had done to me. He made me feel worthless by pressuring me into an abortion, instead of taking on the responsibility like a decent, honorable man should. Now, I had such low self-esteem, I felt unworthy of anyone who would treat me any better.*

*Ultimately, Dave proposed and we got married. We began our marriage with baggage that would take years to sort through. There were constant reminders at every turn: TV commercials, a baby footprint pin on the lapel of a pro-lifer, seeing a newborn baby, the reminders were all around. Eventually, when we had a child, I remember holding my baby boy in my arms, knowing what I had done to my first baby and feeling like I didn't deserve such a beautiful gift.*

*From the day we left that awful facility in 1981 to the fall of 1987 we never talked about the abortion. I suffered in silence, but inside I screamed heartache, anger, regret and sadness, almost each and every day. In June of 1987 we were blessed with a second baby boy. Then, I had difficulties with my third pregnancy and I miscarried. I was heartbroken and wondered if my abortion had caused me to miscarry. I pictured this baby meeting his or her sibling in Heaven and it gave me comfort.*

*In 1987 I attended a Concerned Women for America (CWA) National Convention in Washington D.C. to support Robert Bork, who was nominated to the Supreme Court by President Reagan. My mom was a Regional Director of CWA and she had asked if I was interested in attending with her. I was consumed with trying to protect my secret. I feared that my mom's friends would not accept me and even judge me if they knew my secret. But because of my passion to protect the unborn, I decided to go, even though I knew I would be uncomfortable.*

*When we arrived, we joined with other women making signs, which we would hold while marching on the Capitol steps the next day. I felt like a hypocrite. But, I also felt like I was doing a good thing.*

*On the third day of the convention, a woman spoke at the breakfast meeting. She had adopted a baby that was close to being aborted. She told the story of her adopted baby girl almost being a victim of abortion. Then, she began singing a song she had written about her daughter called, "I Almost Didn't Know You." I started feeling sick to my stomach. I worked hard holding back the tears, but I knew I couldn't, so I excused myself telling my Mom I wasn't feeling well. When I reached the hallway the tears began to flow. In my room I couldn't stop sobbing.*

*The story and the song this woman had shared reminded me that I DIDN'T get to know my baby. Was it a baby girl? Would she have had blue eyes? Blonde hair? Would she have loved to dance, or sing, or both?*

*Was it a baby boy? Would he have loved science or sports, race cars or history? I would never know.*

*On the flight home, my mom began recounting the conference. She still didn't know I had aborted her grandchild. She didn't know the pain I was carrying. I struggled to carry on a normal conversation, like everything was fine, but I was overwhelmed with sadness and shame.*

*On my first day back home, after my husband left for work, I was thinking about my experience at the Convention. I was glad I had gone. I remember being alone in the living room. I closed the curtains. I cried out to God for forgiveness. Tears began flowing. How could I continue with this internal pain? I felt so alone and so sad.*

*But God spoke to me that morning. I heard Him tell me in that moment of my agony that He was going to use me for His glory. It's not like I heard Him audibly, but He spoke to my mind, my heart, and my soul. I didn't really know what it meant, but I believed that somehow and someday God would use me, even if it was only to help just one person. I felt God tell me that it was time to take a baby step toward healing.*

*The next day I said to my husband, "We have to talk about the abortion. It happened. We've swept it under the rug all these years and we're not going to make it in our marriage unless we talk about what we did." This was the first time in over six years that I had even spoken the word, "abortion." The pretending needed to end. All those years, I would sit in church and look around thinking that I was the only woman in church who had had an abortion. I felt so bad about myself all the time. It was way past time to seek help. Dave agreed to try to get help. We went to our first counseling session. It was the first step toward seeking healing and Dave and I were actually talking about the abortion.*

*In 1988, I became pregnant again, not too long after my miscarriage. I started experiencing problems and learned that one of my baby's kidneys was not functioning properly. After countless trips to see my doctor, 24 ultra-sounds later, and residing near the hospital for the final four* weeks of my pregnancy, I gave birth to our third baby boy. Again, I wondered if any of the complications were the result of the abortion.

Over the next few years, Dave focused on work and supporting our family and I focused on doing what moms do. We found a church home where we attended a few more counseling sessions. These loving, caring, godly men tried to help us, but they weren't trained to work with post-abortive women and men.

At that time, no one knew about my abortion except for the counselors we had gone to. One Sunday an ad in the bulletin about a "post-abortive support group" caught my attention. It was to be held at the local Crisis Pregnancy Center (CPC). My dilemma was that I knew the Director of CPC very well and she did not know that I had had an abortion. Also, my Mom's best friend served on the CPC Board and she didn't know about my abortion either. Finally, with God's leading, I decided to tell them about my abortion. The time came and I was so fearful, but God gave me courage. I started crying as I shared my story. I was afraid they would reject and judge me. Instead they cried with me. They prayed over me and I left feeling loved and encouraged. I attended that first class, taking another step toward healing.

Shortly after that, I attended a new Bible study that was offered at CPC for post-abortive women. I learned more deeply about God's grace and His love for me on a fresh and new level. While I was indeed accountable for what I had done, God wanted me to accept the gifts He was offering me: grace, forgiveness and His unconditional love. God's Word came alive to me and I finally received healing and made peace with God regarding my abortion.

In 2001, God placed on my heart the desire to go through leadership training to help other women find healing through His Word. I thought back to the time in my living room with my curtains drawn, when I cried out to God and He spoke to me about using me to help *others heal. But before going into leadership I would need share my abortion story with those closest to us.*

*Dave and I called a family meeting with our boys. At the time, our three sons were 18, 14 and 12. We were both fearful and didn't know how they would react. I didn't know if they would think less of me. As their mom, I didn't want to let them down. It broke my heart looking at them and knowing it could have been one of them that had been aborted. God gave me peace to finally share our story with our precious boys.*

*Dave talked about his part in the abortion. We wanted them to know that we had messed up...that we were imperfect, but that we had a perfect God who can make all things new. Because of being miles apart, I wrote my parents a letter to share my story. They were loving, forgiving, and supportive. The next time they came to visit they brought me a bouquet of beautiful roses, sending a message of their unconditional love and forgiveness.*

*It is a miracle that Dave and I have now been married for over 32 years. Part of my healing process was focused on forgiveness. We are all called to forgive others for wronging us. God showed me grace and I needed to show grace to my husband. This didn't come naturally! I had some deep-seeded anger to deal with. But God gave me the ability to love Dave unconditionally just as He loves me unconditionally.*

*If I hadn't had Christ in my life to carry me through my darkest days, I most likely would have turned to alcohol, drugs or something worse to mask the pain. I am also thankful to those who prayed for us through those dark times.*

*—Dianne*

## DISCUSS DIANNE'S STORY

1. In what ways can you identify with Dianne's story? What were you feeling?

2. What did Dianne do to promote her post-abortive healing process?

3. In what ways does reading Dianne's story give you hope and comfort?

## ANGER

Anger is a very personal emotional response that exhibits frustration and agitation over a situation that we can no longer change. Anger usually focuses on what is past—on something that already happened. Anger displays antagonism toward others over hurt or frustration that we are feeling, whether those individuals have anything to do with our hurt and frustration or not.

Many women respond to their abortion with anger. In many cases, we may not even know why we're angry. Perhaps we've never even associated our anger with our abortion.

As post abortive women, we often feel angry at ourselves, at those who coerced us into an abortion, at those who participated in any way, and at those who failed to intervene and provide a way out. We may also be angry at the circumstances leading up to and resulting from our abortion. Often, we may be angry with God for allowing this to happen, even though we must admit our part in it.

Of all the emotions we feel, anger is one of the most dangerous and volatile. Anger is a desperate attempt to regain control over a situation in which we feel we've lost control. As a result, we lash out at ourselves or others. Anger provokes irrational and unhealthy thoughts, words, and behavior.

Anger is also very contagious and destroys relationships. For example, in our anger over our abortion, we may lash out at a loved one who just happens to be nearby. Perhaps we don't feel *worthy* of love, so why should this person love us? In our anger, we push them away rejecting their love and denying them ours.

Anger often causes us to do things contrary to our conscience and moral standards. Anger can lead to self-destructive behaviors like: drinking, drugs, sexual escapades, binge eating, unrestrained gambling, and all sorts of other behaviors that only worsen our situation. In cases of self-abuse, we subconsciously direct our anger toward ourselves as punishment for what we've done or failed to do.

Anger is an emotion that we *yield* to. We feel justified in being angry. We give anger free reign and let it dictate our responses to life. This is scary. When anger is in control, we cannot heal and we injure others. Anger is like acid that eats away at the person holding it.[20] The awful things we think and say about ourselves become self-fulfilling prophecies.

Anger, if unrestrained, consumes our life. Anger weaves strong patterns in our lives that are difficult to break. We're angry over our abortion and we look for things around us to justify and feed our anger. For this reason, we must recognize that the thing we're angry at in the moment may not be the source or root of our anger—our abortion.

Over time, various responses to our abortion may include: *hiding, denying, blaming,* and *rationalizing* or *justifying*. Anger may be a common emotion for us in any and all of these responses.

## HOW DO WE GET RID OF ANGER?

In order to break the patterns of anger in our lives, we must identify its root cause. Anger is a very *relational* response. What that means is that even if we are angry over a situation or an event, we invariably direct our anger toward *people*. This may be ourselves, God, anyone else who was involved in our abortion, or we may take out our anger on those around us who have nothing to do with our abortion. Anger expresses itself toward people.

Because of this relational aspect of anger, the only way to truly rid ourselves of anger is to forgive those who have offended us—including ourselves. When we're angry at someone, we put the onus on them to change, not realizing that *we* need to change. *We* must take the initiative. *Forgiveness is vital, because it removes the reason for our anger.* For some of us, forgiving others and ourselves may be extremely difficult.

First, we may think that if we forgive someone for their role in our pregnancy or abortion that we are somehow condoning their actions. This is not true. In reality, the act of forgiveness *validates* that there is a real offense which warrants forgiving.

Second, we mistakenly think that by withholding forgiveness from someone, we exercise control over them. We may think that by not forgiving them, we continue to hold something over them. This is a form of revenge. The irony is that withholding forgiveness from others harms *us* more than it harms them. Someone has wisely said, "Refusal to forgive someone is like drinking poison and hoping the other person suffers."

Finally, forgiveness is often difficult for us because we have held onto anger for so long it has become a part of us. Anger has woven its patterns into our life. We may even feel that parting with our anger will strip us of something dear to us. This thinking is part of the folly of anger. It is irrational and controls us. It's like keeping a rabid dog in the basement that we continue to feed, even though we're afraid of it. But we will only find relief when we remove the cause of our anger.

We cannot go back and erase our abortion, but we can forgive others and ourselves for our role in it. Doing so will help us end the awful rule of anger in our lives.

## TAKE ACTION: STEPS TO FORGIVING OTHERS

1. **Identify those with whom you are angry.** Write down here everyone who was involved in your abortion and toward whom you may be directing anger. (Include anyone and everyone that even remotely had a role in your abortion, including yourself.)




2. **Forgive each of these individuals.** We are not suggesting that you actually go to each of these individuals or even call or write them. (In some cases, you may choose to do so, but not for everyone.) There are two parts to this step:

    a. **Prepare a short statement that you will actually speak aloud.** This statement may say something like: "_____ (person's name), I forgive you for your role in my abortion and I release my grudge against you."

    b. **Speak these words of forgiveness for each person on your list.** Go somewhere private to do this. Work through your list and speak your statement of forgiveness aloud in your own hearing. Saying it aloud is important because it helps validate the act and demands that you speak it in a way that you mean it.

3. **Next, understand that anger is a two-way street.** People have offended us and therefore we are angry. Remember, as long as we hold onto anger it controls and poisons us. Forgiving others is the key to freedom from anger.

    But *we* have offended others as well (through aborting our child, or by the way we've treated them post-abortion). So too, if we have offended others, we can find refreshment and freedom by going to them and asking their forgiveness. By taking initiative to ask their forgiveness, we also offer them freedom from their anger.

    You must approach this step using some common sense:

    a. **Make this a short list.** Who are the people that really matter in your life? Have you offended them? If so, go to them and ask them to forgive you. As I write this, I know a woman who aborted her child without the father's knowledge. He was very hurt by her act and now she deeply regrets her abortion as well. She needs his forgiveness and he needs to forgive her.

    b. **Choose your words wisely.** Words like, "Sorry if I offended you," can sound insincere and hypocritical. Say something like, "I'm sorry I offended you. Would you please forgive me?" If you feel you need to provide the person with the context for your apology, then do so.

4.  **Consider asking God to forgive you.** As you read this, you will know whether this step is right for you now. If you would like to ask God's forgiveness for your abortion and other actions that have followed as a result, simply talk to Him and tell Him you're sorry and ask Him to forgive you. God loves it when we come to Him like this. He will not turn you away or deny you forgiveness.

5.  **Be prepared for reappearances of anger.** Because anger may have been your companion for many years, it will try to come back and take hold of you again. That's why it's important to record above what you have done: whom you've forgiven and what you said. Then, when anger does raise its ugly head again, come back to what you did in this exercise. You may need to do this from time to time.

    Some people experience an immediate and complete sense of release and freedom in forgiveness. With others it occurs over time. If you're one of those who continues to struggle with anger and forgiveness, don't be discouraged or frustrated, but keep at it. Come back to actions you initiated in this exercise. Keep rehearsing the truth of what you know.

## SESSION SIX

PAULA'S STORY

**Please read the following true story and reflect on the questions that follow.**

*Many years ago, I was serving in the US Marine Corps. One day I accepted a ride home from one of the soldiers that I worked with. As a result of allowing myself to get into this situation, he violently raped me. When I got back to the barracks I was in a state of shock. Because of his threats I was afraid to tell anyone, but felt tremendous guilt and shame.*

*Three months went by and I still hadn't told anybody, but I could no longer ignore the fact that I was pregnant. On our base there was a club for enlisted personnel that was run by a couple. They took many of us under their wing kind of like surrogate parents. I told this woman I was pregnant and she went with me to the doctor to confirm my pregnancy.*

*At this point, I called my parents and my mom flew down and went to the doctor with me for a checkup. I knew at the time that I didn't want an abortion. I felt that abortion was wrong. Many talk about "justifiable abortion" due to the fact that I was raped and by a man of another race. But to me abortion was not justifiable. My mom was very supportive and put no pressure on me either way.*

*When we got back to the barracks my dad called me. I loved my dad. He was my idol. I adored and worshiped him. But over the phone he broke down and began crying. He said he didn't know how the family could deal with this. Well that destroyed me and I decided then and there to abort the baby.*

*I went to the Navy hospital for the procedure. They led me into a room that wasn't even an operating room, but more like a large office. Because a Navy hospital is also a training facility, the doctor conducting the abortion had 8 or 9 other doctors in training in the room with me. He proceeded to explain to them about the procedure and what he was going to do to me.*

*Being treated like this was terribly humiliating, shameful and embarrassing. They gave absolutely no thought for what I might be feeling or going through under the circumstances. They were so callous and cold. I had no friends or family there to stay with me.*

*The doctor told me in a cold, clinical fashion what to expect and the nurse was even colder. He said that because I was so far along, they couldn't perform a simple D&C, but would have to inject a saline solution into my uterus to end the life of the fetus. After doing so, they sent me to a hospital room and told me to get up on my own to go to the bathroom if I had the urge.*

*I was so young, naïve and ignorant at the time. After a while I got up to go to the bathroom and gave birth to the fetus in the toilet. I experienced utter horror and didn't know what to do. I felt like I was in a nightmare in another world. My heart was broken. A piece of me died that day.*

*Just then the nurse came in, took a look and said, "I'll take care of that." She sent me back to my bed and retrieved the fetus. She didn't tell me what gender it was. She didn't tell me anything.*

*At the time, I had a hard time calling it a baby, because that made it too real.*

*After this ordeal, the Marine Corps gave the option to either remain active duty or to leave and go back home. I chose to go home. At home we never spoke about the abortion. I knew my mom felt guilty about it. I felt like I was in a fog.*

*My self-esteem plummeted to zero. I carried horrible guilt and anger. I was angry at God for allowing this all to happen. I was so desperate for someone to love me and make me feel worthy. I just felt so unworthy of love or anything good.*

*Around this time I met my first husband. I saw him as my savior—someone to love me. In my mind he loved me. But we really struggled in our marriage and I never told him about the rape or abortion. After two years we decided to have a child in spite of our marriage difficulties. I was scared to death that I'd never be able to have children again as judgment for killing my baby.*

*But I did get pregnant. However, I began having complications early in my pregnancy with bleeding. And I thought, "God is punishing me." At seven months, my husband and I were still having problems and he left me. He had done many things that made me feel so unworthy of love or anything good.*

*I went in at seven months for another appointment and asked the doctor if my baby was going to be alright. He said, "I'm concerned about both of you." Both the baby and I were in a bad way physically. I cried out to God, "Just let my baby live and I'll do anything."*

*Little Travis was born two months premature. He was very tiny, but he survived. During this time I was very down. Carrying the weight of the rape, the abortion and now my divorce, I was at the lowest point I had been. Several times I contemplated suicide. Had it not been for little Travis, I may have gone through with it.*

*Over the next three years, my parents helped me get into a house and I got a job. At this point, my emotions swung the opposite direction and I decided I didn't need anyone. "I can do this myself," I thought.*

*But after some time, I met my current husband and we married after three months. He loved me unconditionally even though I felt so unworthy of his love. Because of me I don't know how we made it through our first year of marriage, but my husband just kept loving me in spite of what I said or did. His unconditional love served as the initial catalyst for my post-abortion healing.*

*My husband had been in the military, was out when we married, but decided to reenlist. We were soon transferred to Hawaii. One day in Hawaii, I was sitting in an enlisted club with two other women. The three of us were talking and, on a whim, decided to start reading the Bible together. We didn't really know what we were doing, but through it began drawing near to God. I was still carrying around a lot of guilt and shame at the time.*

*About four years into our marriage, my mom sent me a tape from a speaker named Rachel Johnson. She did a lot of counseling of post-abortive women. On this tape, she encouraged me to imagine the following scene: I saw myself standing in a beautiful field full of wild flowers, with a gentle breeze blowing and the sun shining.*

*Then I visualized a figure coming toward me from far across the field. As this figure drew closer, I could tell that it was an adult with a child. As they continued walking toward me, I recognized that it was Jesus. He walked up to me and placed the child's hand in my hand. Then he said, "I have your child. I'm holding her for you until you come."*

*I never knew what the gender of my aborted baby had been, but from that moment forward I knew it was a girl. This experience totally broke me and set me free from my guilt and shame. I felt completely safe and accepted by Jesus.*

*Rachel also encouraged me to look at myself as I would look at another young woman who might be in my situation. I knew I would accept her and extend grace, mercy and forgiveness to that young woman, so I should do the same toward myself.*

*Some years later, I was meeting with 12 other women and someone shared a personal experience that prompted me to tell the story of my rape and abortion. This was the first time I had shared my story. I was amazed that day at two things. I was amazed that my story encouraged the other women so much. But I was also amazed to learn that at least three quarters of those women had experienced rape, sexual abuse or abortion.*

*Mine was no isolated case. There are thousands of women who have had similar experiences. Since that time, I have given my time and energy to helping other women heal from the wounds of their abortions. I am amazed that God has entrusted me with this task. He truly does love and accept me just like I am with all the junk from my past.*

*—Paula*

## DISCUSS PAULA'S STORY

1. In what ways can you identify with Paula's story? What were you feeling?

2. What did Paula do to process her abortion?

3. In what ways does reading Paula's story give you hope and comfort?

## FEAR

Whereas anger focuses on what is past, fear is anxious about what *could* happen in the future. Like anger, fear is an emotion to which we relinquish power. When we yield to fear, we grant it permission to rule over us and control us. Fear may have caused us to hide, deny, or blame someone else for our abortion.

Fear can be crippling and paralyzing. Fear can prevent us from making good decisions or making any decisions at all. To some extent, fear probably played a role in our abortion. If so, our fear drove us to do something that we now deeply regret. Our abortion also spawned a situation that causes us to fear in a variety of ways.

Please check any of the things below that have evoked fear in your life. As post-abortive women, we may have harbored fears about:

☐ Being found out

☐ The long-term consequences resulting from our abortion

☐ Whether people will reject us

☐ Whether God will punish us for what we did

☐ Whether God would ever trust us or allow us to have children

☐ Whether our children will repeat the same mistakes we've made

☐ Other: _____

_____

Lest there be any confusion, keep in mind that there are different kinds of *fear*. For instance, we can have a healthy fear of dark alleys at night that prompts us to take proper precautions. We also may cultivate a healthy fear of failure that motivates us to show up at work on time and perform our jobs well. A soldier experiences a healthy fear when going into battle and overcomes that fear with courage and training.

But the kind of fear we're talking about here is neither healthy nor overcome with safeguards. The fear we're talking about haunts and cripples us. This form of fear is unhealthy, destructive and prevents our healing. The antidote for this kind of fear is... *love and acceptance*.

Imagine that you're a little girl and you awake from a terrifying nightmare in the middle of the night. You cry out and your mom or dad hears you, comes in and sits down on your bed and holds you, comforting you and rocking you in their strong arms. Held in their embrace, all your fears melt away. *Love dispels fear.*

While little girls have little fears, grown women can have big fears. Fear steals our joy and paralyzes us. Fear keeps us from taking risks and entering new relationships. Left unchecked, fear begins to influence our every decision. Fear can run and ruin our life.

## HOW DO WE STOP BEING FEARFUL?

Our fear of being rejected by others is fueled by our refusal to allow others to love us. Ironically, our fear often causes us to push them away. We may reject their love because we feel so unworthy. Or perhaps we've been burned so many times we fear being hurt again, so we withhold our love from others.

It is true, every time we love someone and allow them to love us, we run the risk of being disappointed, abandoned, or hurt. Still, we desperately need the love of others in our lives. *To love and be loved is a basic human need.* When we allow fear to keep us from love, we give it permission to deny us a basic human need. As long as we're fearful, we cannot heal.

When we allow fear to prevent us from trusting others, we'll never experience their love—the very thing that will dispel our fear. This is one reason we discussed forgiveness last week. By forgiving others and asking their forgiveness, we have opened the door for reconciliation, trust and real love.

In a very real way, we must deal with our irrational fears *rationally*. That is, we must face them with courage. We must decide to take a risk and allow others to love us. We must risk loving them. We must weigh this decision carefully and wisely. We don't want to abandon ourselves to someone who does not truly love us. We all know too well how poorly that will go.

A word of caution: people will pretend to love you because they want something from you. What people want from you could include money, sex, attention, domestic services, admiration or approval. Before exposing yourself to another person, take time to consider this question:

*Would this person truly love me as I really am if I did not have* _____*to offer them?*

Choose wisely. There are those who do love you dearly. Abandon yourself to their love first. Let them love and comfort you and return their love freely.

TAKE ACTION: THREE STEPS FOR BECOMING FREE FROM FEAR:

1. **Make a list of people who truly love you just as you are.** These people love you unconditionally with no strings attached.

2. **From that list of people who love you, identify the person with whom you could most likely be a confidant.** This is someone you can trust, who loves you and you love them. Don't think of romantic love in this context. This person could be your spouse, but most of us also need another woman in our lives in whom we can confide. I cannot emphasize how important this is for your emotional, social, and spiritual health!

   We must be very picky about who we choose for a confidant. Look for someone you look up to. Choose a woman who doesn't necessarily have it all together, but she's also not on the brink of disaster. You're not looking for a "project" here, and neither should she.

   Simply ask this person if they would start meeting with you regularly (we recommend weekly). Share the characteristics of a confidant with them below, so you're both on the same page. Commit to confidentiality and transparency. Then establish when and where you'll meet.

   Be very intentional about establishing this relationship. You may already know this person,

but have never thought of them as a confidant.
Consider "up-grading" your current relationship.
As you form this relationship, speak openly about
the characteristics you would like to see in this
relationship. Confidants:

a.   **Spend time together in real life.** Let your
     confidant into the whole of your life. If you only
     see each other once a week in a coffee house,
     you won't really get to know each other. You
     have to be able to let your hair down with this
     person and be yourself without condemnation.

b.   **Love and care for each other.** Look for ways to
     serve each other that will clearly demonstrate the
     genuineness of your love and care for each other.

c.   **Challenge each other boldly.** We are often timid
     about pointing out a caustic behavior in another
     person. But if we give each other permission
     to do this at the outset of our relationship, we
     will experience a much richer, more meaningful
     relationship that helps both of us grow as
     individuals.

d.   **Encourage each other in your spiritual journey.**
     Wherever you are in your journey regarding
     faith in God, you want someone who will
     move you forward rather than stifle or hinder
     you. Don't give up ground you've gained with
     God on behalf of someone else's relationship.
     If the other person asks for that concession,
     this should serve as a red flag concerning the
     authenticity of their love.

e.  **Celebrate one another's joys and victories.** Avoid spending time with each other merely complaining, grousing, criticizing others, or gossiping.

3.  **Seek out a healthy group of like-minded people.** These are largely lacking in our society today, but they do exist and can be developed. We need a small group of individuals with whom we can be ourselves and not be guarded all the time. We need people with whom we can have fun, love and be loved.

    Warning! You probably won't find this group of people in a bar! Also, stay clear of groups who find pleasure in gossiping, back-biting, or living shallow lives. You might find a healthy group of people to spend time with in:

    a.  A recovery group like this

    b.  In a common-interest club or association

    c.  A group of peers from work

    d.  A church

For some, the painful reality may be that you couldn't think of any names to write down in Step 1. Or perhaps you wrote down a few names, but there is no one on the list with whom you could be a confidant. If this is the case for you, it will only serve to intensify your pain and increase your fear. This is no way to live your life, so we will speak about this in more detail next week. There are always other options. There's always hope.

## SESSION SEVEN

### CELESTE'S STORY

**Please read the following true story and reflect on the questions that follow.**

*In 1969 I was attending college and had been dating a guy for three years. At the beginning of summer break, I found out I was pregnant. I confided in my older sister who immediately insisted that I get an abortion.*

*She also told my dad. My dad had been a military chaplain and was now a university professor and I had always valued his opinion. He also advised me, "You are young and not married. Your whole life is before you. Finish college, get married and have your babies later." So, I just accepted what he said.*

*Back in 1969, abortion was illegal in my state, so my plan was to go to Tijuana, Mexico for the procedure. But I ended up talking with a local doctor who urged me not to go out of the country for the abortion. Instead, he began probing me with questions like: "How do you feel about getting an abortion?" "What emotional strain might it put on you?" "What if your mom found out about the abortion?" "If your mom found out and was very upset with you, are you prone to thoughts of suicide?"*

*Later, I realized that he was trying to build a case for a medically necessitated abortion. He really wanted to perform this abortion and was willing to stretch the limits of the law to justify it "for my health." He presented his case to a board of physicians in order to gain their approval.*

*I had the abortion and felt no immediate emotional regrets. Yet, I must have felt something, because I wanted to quietly say, "Good bye and I'm sorry," to my baby. So I asked the doctor, "May I see my baby?" But he firmly said, "No, of course not."*

*My dad died about six months after my abortion.*

*Ten years passed and I was now dating a different guy. My period was late and I was sure I was pregnant again. This time I knew I couldn't bring myself to have an abortion. I decided that if I was indeed pregnant, in spite of how it might change the plans I had for my life, I would keep this child. That would be a better option than to live with myself for having killed another child. So I planned to keep my baby. But as it turned out, I wasn't pregnant after all.*

*In 1982, I married my husband Tony. Then, three years later both of us stepped into a personal relationship with God through Jesus Christ. Jesus changed our lives profoundly! I can't imagine how life would be today without Him in our lives.*

*Several years later, I found out that my dad had been a dedicated communist. Pieces of the puzzle began to fall into place and I realized that he had deceived our family in order to take us down a completely different philosophical and spiritual road. That road of socialistic "choices" and* actions had led to negative consequences and brought me a lot of sad times and bad memories.

My dad had guided me into the killing of my child, but I also had a choice in the matter. From the time I found out why he had led me astray in so many areas of my life, I couldn't mourn for him anymore. He had failed as a dad to teach me right from wrong. So many years had been wasted following his advice.

Tony and I had been trying to get pregnant, but couldn't. I was 35 by now and getting concerned. At 37, we heard about a "drug baby," so we adopted this little boy, but still tried to get pregnant. One day when our adopted boy was two years old, a married friend of mine told me she had gotten pregnant and was going to abort her child. I begged her not to, telling her she would deeply regret it later. We even offered to adopt her baby, but she refused our offer and aborted her child.

About that time, I was starting to hear about the pain and torture that happens to a child during an abortion. Those facts and my friend's abortion drove home to me for the first time the horrors of what I had done to my child. I crumpled onto the kitchen floor and wept my eyes out over my aborted baby.

My little boy walked over to me, took my face in his little hands and urged, "Don't cry mommy! Don't cry mommy!" His tender pleadings only magnified the pain of what I had done. Here was our little boy who'd been given to us, and he had almost been aborted by the insistence of his birth mother's family and friends. Here was my baby, ALIVE, because of another desperate woman's difficult choice! My son, Tony and I can never thank her enough for giving him life!

As I continued to read my Bible and got to know the character and love of Jesus, I knew that Christ's sacrifice for me was more than sufficient to cover my sin and that He had forgiven me, but I was still deeply saddened over what I had done.

*Five years later I finally got pregnant and we eventually had two more children—a boy and a girl. I was 42 and 44 years old giving birth to them. I didn't have an amniocentesis. I knew that even if there was something wrong with them, they would be a blessing and God would help me through anything.*

*As they grew into their teen years, I was so ashamed of my past that I told them I had kept myself pure until marriage. I so desperately wanted to be a good role model for them, so they wouldn't follow the way I had gone, which would lead to unnecessary pain.*

*I desperately wanted to volunteer at a local pregnancy center, where I hoped I could counsel young girls who had gotten pregnant not to abort their babies. But I was fearful that some of those girls might know my sons and daughter and that word would get back to my children that I too had had an abortion. So my fear and shame kept me from pursuing this work.*

*Finally, when my daughter was 19, I confessed to her my former lifestyle and abortion. She accepted me and appreciated that I had shared with her. I have also told both my boys.*

*My baby would've been born in March of 1970. I can't tell you how I know, but I see him as a boy. I often wonder what life would've been like with him; what he'd be like as an adult. What I did to him and not being able to know him still makes me very sad. Our culture has duped us and I made a terrible mistake which I'll never forget! But I know that my boy has forgiven me and that God loves me and has forgiven me too.*

*My favorite passage from the Bible is Psalm 139:13-14, "For you created my inmost being; You knit me together in my mother's womb. I praise You because I am fearfully and wonderfully made." I think of my unborn child when I read those verses. God is still in the process of healing me and I truly hope that my story will help heal other women as well.*

*—Celeste*

## DISCUSS CELESTE'S STORY

1. In what ways can you identify with Celeste's story?

2. What triggered Celeste's regret over her abortion?

3. How did Celeste process her abortion?

4. What can you take away from her story that may help you heal?

## SHAME

Shame is a painful emotion caused by a sense of guilt. Shame is a natural and appropriate response to something we've done wrong. The purpose of shame is not to torment us, but to cause us to change. People have a variety of responses to shame. Some may try to "stuff" or "cover" it, while others "beat themselves up" with it, because they feel they deserve it.

Shame is a very common emotion felt by post-abortive women. Shame, like some of the other emotions we've covered, causes us to hide, deny, blame others, or rationalize our decision to abort our child. Shame too is debilitating and will prevent us from healing.

Above all, shame breeds a sense of unworthiness. Many post-abortive women express that after their abortion they feel unworthy of the things listed below. Please check all that apply or have applied to you. Many post-abortive women feel unworthy of:

☐ Having children

☐ Being loved by a good man

☐ Experiencing love and acceptance from others

☐ Receiving or experiencing anything good in life

☐ Other: _____
   _____

One way to look at shame and recognize what it does to us is by the following diagram.[20]

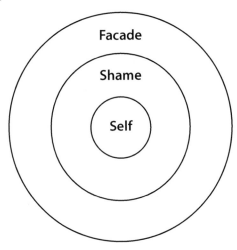

At the center of these concentric circles is our "self" – who we really are. But our shame causes us to hide. By hiding our true self, we cannot be known by others. But in order to establish and maintain relationships, others need to get to know us.[22] So we put up a façade—a false self—to present to others in hopes of being loved and accepted.

The problem is that we all know when someone is putting up a false front. We recognize that what they're showing us is not genuine. Others see this in us too. The result is shallow relationships built on pretense. Our shame literally prevents us from loving others fully or being loved by them.

The key is to deal with our shame, so we can drop the façade and let others in. In this way, we too can begin to love again and be loved. So how do we deal with our shame?

At AbAnon, we have found that many women deal with their shame and find healing from their abortions through a relationship with God. For this reason, even though we do not identify ourselves as a religious organization, we would be remiss if we did not share with you this important remedy for finding freedom from guilt and shame. In the spirit of this, please read the true story we've provided below of another woman.

John, one of Jesus' disciples and an eyewitness, tells about a woman that Jesus met one day. Jesus and His disciples were on foot about half-way into a 75-mile hike from one part of Israel to another. At noon, they stopped at a well in a region called Samaria. Samaria was populated by a people with mixed blood of Jews and non-Jews. Their religious beliefs represented a polluted blend of Judaism and paganism. As a result, most Jews looked down on Samaritans and would have nothing to do with them. But Jesus was different.

Jesus sat by this well in Samaria while His disciples went off to buy food. While they were gone, a Samaritan woman came to draw water from the well. The customs of the day give us insight into this situation. Normally, the women in a village would come to the well in the cool of the morning. They would also use that time to socialize with each other and catch up on the village news.

This woman, however, came to the well at noon. As far as we know, no one else but Jesus was there. We soon become aware of why she chose to come to the well at an hour when she would not have to interact with the other village women.

Jesus initiated the conversation by asking this woman for a drink—which shocked her—because most Jews would never stoop to request anything of a Samaritan. When she expressed her surprise over His request, Jesus said, "If you only knew the gift God has for you and who you are speaking to, you would ask me, and I would give you living water." (John 4:10 NLT)[23]

The woman was confused at Jesus' response at first and thought He was talking about water from the well. But Jesus explained, "Anyone who drinks this water [from the well] will soon become thirsty again. But those who drink the water I give will never be thirsty again. It becomes a fresh, bubbling spring within them, giving them eternal life." (John 4:13-14 NLT)

This offer intrigued the woman and she asked Jesus to give her this ever-thirst-quenching water. Appropriate for the culture of the day, Jesus asked her to go get her husband and come back and Jesus would fill her request. At this point the woman's shame subtly came to light, for she replied, "I have no husband."

Jesus, knowingly responded to her, "You are right when you say you have no husband. The fact is, you have had five husbands, and the man you now have is not your husband. What you have just said is quite true." (John 4:17-18 NIV)[24]

If it weren't for what follows, we might assume that Jesus was being cruel in revealing this woman's shameful secret. Now we understand that the shame of her lifestyle prevented her from coming to the well to draw water in the morning with the other village women. Her shame caused her to come alone in the heat of the day and to bear her burden in solitude.

But in the discussion that followed, Jesus revealed to her that He is the long-awaited Savior and that He was offering her forgiveness of sins and eternal life. The woman was so excited about this that she left her water jar at the well and ran back into the village. She went to everyone she could find and said, "Come and see a man who told me everything I ever did!" (John 4:29 NLT)

At first, her excitement might be mistaken for Jesus' ability to super-naturally see into her past, but that's not what thrilled her so. We read on, "Many of the Samaritans from that town believed in him because of the woman's testimony, "Come and see a man who told me every-thing I ever did!"

What excited her so and moved her to tell others about was that Jesus knew everything there was to know about her past—*and yet He still loved her and offered her the living water of forgiveness and eternal life.* Her unspoken testimony was, "Come see a man who knows every sin I've ever committed, and yet He still loves and accepts me!"

That was not some psychic trick that Jesus pulled when He told this woman about her whole life. He knew her just as thoroughly as He knows you and me. He knows everything you and I have ever done. He knows about our abortions. And He makes that same offer of for-giveness to you and me today. He knows our shame and offers to remove it from us.

## TAKE ACTION

Shame causes us to hide, deny, blame others and justify our abortion. In shame we provide others with a façade, because we are ashamed to reveal our true self. Unless dealt with, shame will prevent us from ever healing or experiencing meaningful relationships. Ironically, shame prevents us from exposing our abortion, but it's only by exposing our abortion that we gain freedom from shame.

*Hiding our shame magnifies it and prolongs our agony. When we reveal and renounce our shame, we find forgiveness and healing.*

Like that Samaritan woman long ago, many post-abortive women have found freedom from guilt and shame by trusting Jesus Christ and receiving His forgiveness. If you would like to trust Jesus Christ and receive His forgiveness, simply pray to Him. Confess your sins to Him and ask Him to forgive you. He doesn't turn anyone away. He loves you and offers you healing.

If as a result of reading this you have put your trust in Christ, please tell your facilitator that you have made this decision. Regardless of whether you choose to put your trust in Christ, we are here to love you and walk with you through your healing process.

## SESSION EIGHT

### KELLY'S STORY

**Please read the following true story and reflect on the questions that follow.**

*My husband and I had been married for only a few months. We had met in college and lived together for five years before we married. We lived a very unhealthy lifestyle—partying all the time and living from paycheck to paycheck.*

*When we found out that I was pregnant, both of us had the same reaction. We immediately thought, "We can't afford a baby! This doesn't fit our lifestyle." At the time we didn't think we ever wanted kids, but at any rate we didn't feel ready now.*

*So we decided we had to "take care of this problem." We never discussed other options. We were too entrenched in our life of partying and having fun.*

*I looked in the Yellow Pages to find a clinic and just chose the first one and made an appointment. I met with a woman there who showed me pictures of the development of a fetus. She was calm, soothing and not at all judgmental or mean. But I realized she was trying to talk me out of my abortion, so I wanted to get out of there.*

*At the time I was young (27) and felt insecure and lacking the confidence to ask questions or counter her arguments. Finally, I stood up and blurted out, "I'm not ready to talk about this anymore," and left.*

*I went back to the Yellow Pages again and found a doctor nearby who performed abortions in his practice. I made an appointment for three or four days later. My husband went with me and the staff was surprised to learn that we were married and seeking an abortion.*

*At the time, I remember feeling distaste for what I was doing. I knew it was wrong, but our independence and finances trumped the baby. My strong feminism also played a role in my decision.*

*In the doctor's office, the nurse led me back to a room and had me lie down on a table. She began to prepare me verbally telling me what to expect: what I would hear, feel and see.*

*I cried through the whole process. The nurse asked me, "Are you crying for pain or emotion?" I was not in physical pain, but felt an overwhelming emotional tugging. Meanwhile, my husband held my hand. He was very somber through the whole procedure. The doctor and nurse remained "clinical."*

*My husband took me home and I began cramping severely. I was nauseated and felt terrible. I slept for a day-and-a-half. A girlfriend of mine came over and tried to cheer me up. She totally dismissed the abortion and tried to make me laugh it off, which only made me feel worse.*

*I didn't want to be one of those people who thought abortion was no big deal. I knew it was wrong and it felt very improper to simply dismiss it.*

*A few days later we were supposed to drive up to San Francisco with another couple for an all-day food and wine-tasting event. When we left that morning, I remember feeling very sad. My friend asked me, "Why are you so down?" I said, "Well, you know what happened on Friday!" And she responded, "Get over it! We're going to the city. We're going to have fun!"*

*And I remember looking at her and telling her, "I think God is going to punish me for what I've done and I'm scared about what that's going to look like." She just gave me a blank stare as if to say, "I have no idea what you're talking about." And she just dismissed it.*

*So I decided, "I'm going to buck up and be cheerful and put this out of my mind and at least pretend that I'm having a good time." I was more concerned with ruining their fun and keeping them from having a good time than I was about my own feelings.*

*About 13 years later, I found myself sitting in a church and listening to a message about Jesus Christ dying for my sins and that he offers forgiveness to all who come to him. During the message the pastor distributed little black pieces of paper and a pencil. He asked us to write down any sin that we thought God couldn't possibly forgive us for. The pencil on black paper made the writing nearly invisible.*

*Without hesitation I wrote down, "My abortion" on my piece of paper. Then the pastor told us to get up, take our pieces of paper to a large wooden cross and nail them to the cross. This was to signify that Jesus died for that sin nailing it to the cross and bearing the guilt and shame on my behalf. In that moment I declared that I wanted to follow Jesus. I felt so grateful, so relieved to be forgiven for my abortion!*

*A couple years later and 15 years after my abortion, a friend of mine invited me to a Life Services fundraising event. After the event, on the way home, I shared my story with my girlfriend. She hadn't known about my abortion. She then asked me if I would consider attending a post-abortive support group. I thought, "Why would I want to do that? I'm forgiven, it's all good." But at her prompting, I decided to go.*

*I wasn't fully on board with being in the group until I got there. Hearing the other women's stories made me realize that I had not fully dealt with my abortion. I began to see that there's value—healing—in sharing my story with others and hearing their stories. It was significant for me to see how God was going to redeem, or bring something good from my abortion.*

*While in that support group, I experienced healing from the secret and the shame. Incredibly, I saw that God could even use my abortion for his glory. He is in the life-changing business—he creates beauty from ashes. I was set free. God not only forgave me, but he began to use my story to encourage and heal other women.*

*—Kelly*

## DISCUSS KELLY'S STORY

1.  In what ways can you identify with Kelly's story? What were you feeling?

2.  What did Kelly do to process her abortion?

3.  What can you take away from her story that may help you heal?

## BRINGING CLOSURE TO YOUR GRIEF

Although you may not have thought about your abortion this way in the past, you now recognize that you have lost a loved one. Women who miscarry, especially later in their pregnancy, also experience grief over the loss of their child.

Grief is a natural and healthy response to great loss. Grief expresses itself in sadness, a sense of deep loss, and mourning. Grief may numb us or overwhelm us. We may feel "lost" or experience a profound sense of emptiness.

Normally, when a loved one passes away, we find consolation and closure through a formal memorial service or funeral. Even though it's difficult to attend such an event, the experience helps us come to grips with reality and initiates healing over our grief that otherwise might not occur.

One thing that makes a miscarried baby or an abortion so difficult to heal from is that we are usually denied the opportunity to formally grieve or provide some kind of memorial for that little one. There has been no closure. We grieve internally, but we have no healthy release for our grief.

As we've already noted, our culture suppresses the humanity and personhood of an aborted child. In doing so, this denies us the freedom to grieve and certainly denounces the need to observe some kind of memorial service for our child.

When we speak of "closure" over our grief, this does not mean that we will never grieve again over our lost child. But it does mean that we've initiated a clear course of action to ascribe dignity and worth to our child, thereby giving credence and voice to our grief.

Many post-abortive women have found great release from their grief and sorrow by making a conscious effort to remember their child in a dignified manner—in a way worthy of a human being. There is no recommended protocol for doing this, but it should be something that you feel will be meaningful to you and honoring to your baby.

For example, many women have found closure to their grief by naming their child. Naming the baby attaches personhood to him or her. Other women might plant a tree as a remembrance, give a memorial gift to a charity, buy a solitary rose and dry or press it to preserve it, or purchase a special necklace or ring to wear in remembrance of their child. The important thing is to find something that holds meaning for you.

## THE ETERNAL NATURE OF THE HUMAN SOUL

God reveals in the Bible that death is not final for a human being. We believe that we will see our aborted babies again. And because of Christ's forgiveness, that reunion with our child will be sweet and joyful, not bitter or sorrowful.

In view of this, one other action that has proven very therapeutic and cathartic for post-abortive women is to write a short note or letter to their baby. In it they may express their love and sorrow; ask forgiveness; talk about meeting them one day; and anything else they deem meaningful to write.

Of course, this note or letter won't go anywhere, but it would be one more way of honoring your child and ascribing to him or her their humanity and worth.

TAKE ACTION

We ask that you complete three specific tasks this week. Because of the nature of two of these tasks, you won't want to leave them for the last moment before Session Eight.

1.  Please write a short note or letter to your aborted child or children. This letter or note is for your eyes only, unless you choose to share it with others.

2.  In addition to the note or letter, think of some meaningful way to establish a memorial for your child. This is a very personal exercise. It does not matter what someone else does, you choose something that is most meaningful to you in remembering your child and bringing closure to their death. Some women may wish to perform this exercise with their confidant or another trusted individual.

3.  One of the reasons that our culture fails to recognize the reality of post abortion stress syndrome is the lack of testimony by women who have experienced it.

    Abortion Anonymous and the community of tens of millions of post-abortive women would be very grateful if you would take a few minutes to **complete an anonymous online survey** that we are conducting. This survey will help us demonstrate to the world the harm that abortion causes women. **The survey will only take you a few minutes and is completely anonymous.**

    Please go to the following web address and take this survey *www.AbAnon.org/survey*. Thank you.

## ADDITIONAL STEPS FOR HEALING

Our hope and prayer is that this curriculum has at the very least helped contribute to your healing process. Healing from an abortion is no small matter and often requires more than one or two experiences like this. Please let us know how we can serve you to help further your healing process. Following are some suggested next steps:

1. Continue to meet with your **confidant** on a weekly basis.

2. Meet with a **mentor** for a period of time. A mentor is usually a woman who has been through the AbAnon curriculum and has experienced a measure of healing. She has volunteered to work with other post-abortive women to help them in their healing process.

3. Join another post-abortive **small group** session like this one.

   a. You are welcome to go through this experience again with another group.

   b. Or, we can assist you to find another group with a different curriculum to further promote your healing.

4. If you would like to deepen your relationship with Jesus Christ, please let us know and we can help facilitate this as well.

5. If you would like to hear more about God and Jesus Christ, please let us know and we can provide additional resources and opportunities for you.

# ENDNOTES

1   Guttmacher Institute, "Induced Abortion in the United States," July 2014, http://www.guttmacher.org/pubs/fb_induced_abortion.html.

2   Guttmacher Institute.

3   Guttmacher Institute.

4   Clinic Quotes, "Former Clinic Worker Joan Appleton," September 11, 2012, http://clinicquotes.com/former-clinic-worker-joan-appleton/.

5   Clinic Quotes.

6   Clinic Quotes.

7   Clinic Quotes.

8   Clinic Quotes.

9   Clinic Quotes.

10   Clinic Quotes.

11   National Abortion Federation, "Post-Abortion Syndrome," 2010, https://www.prochoice.org/about_abortion/myths/post_abortion_syndrome.html.

12   Christina Martin, "Tears Streamed Down Her Face as She Talked about Her Abortion, but Abortion Doesn't Hurt Women?" LifeNews.com, July 30, 2014, http://www.lifenews.com/2014/07/30/tears-streamed-down-her-face-as-she-talked-about-her-abortion-but-abortion-doesnt-hurt-women/.

13    Susanne Babbel, PhD, MFT, "Post Abortion Stress Syndrome (PASS) – Does it Exist?" Psychology Today, October 25, 2010, http://www.psychologytoday.com/blog/somatic-psychology/201010/post-abortion-stress-syndrome-pass-does-it-exist.

14    Susanne Babbel.

15    AfterAbortion.com, "What is PASS?" http://afterabortion.com/pass_details.html.

16    AfterAbortion.com.

17    Lee Hudson, *Plains Thunder: the Invitation from Jesus to Real Worship* (Anchorage, AK: Saint Elias Music, LLC, 2011), p. 35.

18    Frederica Mathewes-Green, *Real Choices* (Sisters, OR: Multnomah Books, 1994), p. 19.

19    Over 70% of women who abort, do so against their conscience. David C. Reardon, PhD, p. 191.

20    Based on Mark Twain's quote, "Anger is an acid that can do more harm to the vessel in which it is stored than to anything on which it is poured."

21    Donald Miller, *Scary Close—Dropping the Act and Finding True Intimacy* (Nashville, TN: Nelson Books, 2014), pp. 20ff.

82485988R00062

Made in the USA
San Bernardino, CA
16 July 2018